ANTHONY WILSON

RIDDANCE

First published in 2012 by
Worple Press
Achill Sound
2b Dry Hill Road
Tonbridge
Kent TN9 1LX
www.worplepress.co.uk

Cover image: detail from 'All Lives, All Dances, All is Loud' (mixed
media wall hanging) by Lucy Mason. With kind permission of Greg
Mason.

Printed by imprintdigital
Upton Pyne, Exeter
www.imprintdigital.net

Typeset by narrator
www.narrator.me.uk
enquiries@narrator.me.uk

ISBN: 978-1-905208-16-6

for Merenna and Shimi

Contents

Acknowledgements

Acknowledgments are due to the editors of the following publications, where some of these poems first appeared: *English, English in Education, Magma, The North, The Rialto, Seam, The SHOp, Smiths Knoll, Tall Lighthouse Poetry Review, Third Way, The Use of English.*

A number of these poems appeared in the pamphlet *The Year of Drinking Water* (Exeter Leukaemia Fund, 2007), and were shortlisted in the Poetry Business Book and Pamphlet Competition 2006 and 2008. Various poems also appeared in *Rhyme and Design* (edited by Harry Guest and Peter and Alice Oswald, Peninsula Cancer Network, 2010).

'Chemotherapy' takes its inspiration from a photograph by Annie Leibovitz of Susan Sontag; 'Spooning Couple' takes its title from a sculpture of the same name by Ron Mueck. 'Jem Southam's Photographs' is inspired by a display of 'Josie' and 'Josie, 1992/3' by Jem Southam (Artists Loan Scheme, Exeter Health Care Arts). 'All Lives, All Dances, All is Loud' takes its title and inspiration from a mixed media wall-hanging by the textile artist Lucy Mason, first shown at the Royal Albert Museum and Gallery, Exeter, in 2006.

An earlier version of 'For Afterwards' appeared in *Nowhere Better Than This* (Worple Press, 2002). 'The real reason for working' contains lines from 'Hymn of Life' by James Schuyler, *Collected Poems* (Farrar, Strauss and Giroux, 1993). 'These poems have been arriving each day' borrows from 'Poems' by Raymond Carver, *A New Path to the Waterfall* (Collins Harvill, 1989). 'The bats wheel at head height' borrows from 'During Midnight' (unpublished ms) by Anthony McMahon, and is in memory of him. 'Seller Feedback' contains lines from 'Death by Water' by Robert Bringhurst, *Selected Poems* (Jonathan Cape, 2010). 'To Peter Sansom From a Classroom in Exeter' borrows from 'Use' by Peter Sansom, *Everything You've Heard is True* (Carcanet, 1990) and 'Twelfth Night or What You Will' by Peter Sansom, *Point of Sale* (Carcanet, 2000).

Some of the text of the Introduction first appeared in the Introduction to *The Year of Drinking Water* and 'Poetry Exhaustion' (Smiths Knoll, 2009).

'Teacups' was commissioned by Gwenllian Riall. 'The Ring' was commissioned by Pete James. 'To My Cancer' was commissioned by Ann and Peter Sansom for the 25th Anniversary Edition of *The North*.

Grateful thanks is made to Greg Mason for permission to use a detail of 'All Lives, All Dances, All is Loud' by Lucy Mason for the cover of this book.

I am indebted to Andy Brown, Peter Carpenter, Joanna Cutts, Ann Gray, Mary Jacobs, Michael Laskey, Lawrence Sail, Ann Sansom, Peter Sansom, Jean Sprackland and Christopher Southgate.

I would like to thank all the staff who work on the haematology ward where I was treated.

Introduction

I was formally diagnosed with non-Hodgkin's lymphoma, a cancer of the lymphatic system, on Valentine's Day, 2006. I was 42.

The poems in *Riddance* concern my experience of diagnosis, treatment, misdiagnosis of relapse and remission of and from this increasingly common disease.

I did not begin writing the poems in this book until my treatment for it was nearly complete, in September 2006. It is no accident that this coincided with being able to concentrate again on previously taken-for-granted tasks, such as reading.

Any number of books explain from scientific and personal perspectives what happens when an individual is diagnosed with cancer, but this is not the same thing as describing the truth for the individual who is experiencing it. This is often found in more unexpected places: a nurse's joke as she begins to inject you; a tin of brownies left on the doorstep by a friend; the offer of a lift by a neighbour. Not all of these things appeared in the accounts of cancer that I read before my course of chemotherapy removed my ability to concentrate.

I vowed when my treatment ended not to write but to read again.

Among my favourite books as I rediscovered the pleasure of reading were Julia Darling's two collections of poetry, *Sudden Collapses in Public Places* (2003), and *Apology for Absence* (2004) (both published by Arc). Here at last was a voice I could trust, speaking directly with warmth, wit and a wry mordant humour. Here were poems – yes – about waiting rooms and treatment tables, but also about the joys of listening to Joni Mitchell and sitting in cafés. (Cancer can include these things too).

As I began to recover from my treatment and gain some kind of distance from my experience I felt compelled, emboldened by Darling's example, to seek out metaphors which challenged and subverted the everyday discourse used to describe the disease. Some, the (to me, unhelpful) idea of cancer as a battle

3

('I am Fighting', 'Probably Nothing'), I had heard used, and used myself, before I was ill. Others, such as the idea of winning and losing ('More Chelsea Than Sunderland', 'Acceptance'), I came across serendipitously as it were, in the stories of friends. Other aspects of cancer are explored in the metaphors of transmutation ('Heads', 'Man in a Fleece'); a doomed relationship ('The End of the Affair'); and reincarnation ('I am Becoming My Grandmother').

Sometimes one uses another agency or stimulus that is not at all personal to help shape the material. One looks at a photograph ('Chemotherapy', 'Jem Southam's Photographs'), or a sculpture ('Spooning Couple'); or finds, in a story that is different from one's own, new parallels and resonances ('Jesus Heals Ten Lepers', 'Dr Evil Has Plans for World Domination', 'On Re-reading 'The Man With Night Sweats''). Sometimes it is enough to try to address one's own experience as if it were a person, there in the room with you ('Tumour', 'Wart', 'Blood', 'No', 'To My Cancer').

The poems in the first part of this book were written at great speed in the months of September and October 2006. They have been previously published together as a separate volume (Exeter Leukaemia Fund, 2007) and are reprinted here with kind permission of ELF.

Part Two of *Riddance* is a long poem in memory of my friend Lucy Mason. Lucy was a designer and maker of textile wall-hangings. She was diagnosed with lung cancer a few weeks before I was informed of my own remission. 'All Lives, All Dances, All is Loud' is the title of one of Lucy's final pieces, and takes its title from a forager's song from the part of Devon where she lived.

Lucy endured her illness for over two years with grace, courage and humour, always in hope that she would get better, but always aware she might not. Eventually the news came through that it was a case of when, not if, she would die. I had begun an earlier version of the poem after visiting the Royal Albert Museum and Gallery in Exeter where Lucy was exhibiting her work, in September 2006. Now I felt compelled to complete the poem as a present for her. A race against time, I wrote it in the car, in the dark, during meetings and at mealtimes. I am pleased to say –though relieved is more accurate– that Lucy was able to read the finished poem in the days before even reading was lost to her for good. She died on All Hallows' Eve, 2008.

The poems in Part Three of *Riddance* were written mostly in 2007, as 'normal' life returned. Some were started during the intense period of writing that yielded *The Year of Drinking Water*. Looking at these poems again, I am struck by how many of them deal with the borderlands between different landscapes. Again, I do not think this is surprising: it is quite common to read in the accounts of former cancer patients descriptions of it as a terrain or territory with its own rules and customs which are just as fixed as those found in the so-called 'real' world. The changes in the body, reflected in the natural world, become a space where symbol and reality meet, merge and finally dissolve.

When I began writing these poems the experience I had was one of surprise: I had thought that I had finished writing about my cancer, that there was nothing left to say on the subject.

This is also what I felt while writing the poems in the fourth section of the book, which begins on 'estuary sands' in that uncertain space connecting land, sea and sky. These poems share similar features in that they are very short, do not have titles and recursively explore the liminal terrain between waking and dreaming, work and family, light and dark. They were not written with any particular objective in mind, least of all to plot a linear narrative. Written (again at great speed) during a period of intense pressure at my place of work, I had no sense as I began writing them of the oblique map they make of the tentative territory of remission. Indeed, I thought they formed the start of a new collection of work altogether. I am indebted to Peter Carpenter for his patience as he helped me realise the potential contribution of this section to the book as a whole.

Some of the poems contained in the final section of the book were started in note-form before I was ill. These include

'At Villars', 'Golf at Hawick', 'Against Realism', 'On His Last Ever Drop of Teacher's' and 'Reasons for Life'. Reacquainting myself with them once I was better became a debt of honour to the vocation of writing poetry; I had no real ambitions for them other than to 'finish' them to the best of my ability. They have been placed at the end of this collection because, alongside some newer poems, they are an attempt to recover and celebrate all that seems most essential and affirming about the act of living.

In collecting these poems together I hope I have been able to live up to Stephen Dunn's notion of poetry as a 'corrective': an effort of concentration which refuses to be overwhelmed by circumstances, where one looks for the 'gift' in everything, to use Julia Darling's phrase. I hope they are able, in their own way, to begin and even sustain a conversation about what it is we go through when our lives are touched by cancer. Finally, I hope they help to refresh what we know –or think we do– when we talk about such things, reliant as we are on saying how it was for us, beginning with what happened.

Anthony Wilson

Exeter, 2012

There was one fly
  - Theodore Roethke

One

The Year of Drinking Water

Tumour

You gave me time to notice –
apple blossom, hand movements,
the light taking leave of rooms.
I would like to claim
new attention to my children
but the truth is they grew up
whether I watched them or not.
Mostly I slept.
You began in midsummer.
It took till February to find you.
By then all I knew were symptoms:
insomnia, night sweats, a cough
I could not shake off.
Because of you I revisited old LPs –
I did not want to die
not having fried onions to Grover,
made bubbles to This Mortal Coil.
The script writers of *Frasier*
helped me recover from you,
plus condensed milk and broccoli –
though not at the same time.
Eventually I drank coffee again.
You reacquainted me with my guilt –
the way I glared at S
after she'd poured out her heart
in the autumn of endless nights
with nothing but the wind for company.
I chose songs, having you,
and invented ceremonies by rivers.
(But I found no poetry in you.)

You saved me from talking about house prices.
You obliterated my craving for alcohol.
I would say I am grateful
but am not ready for that, just yet.

How to Pray for the Dying

Do not say: 'Lord, this is not of you,'
rebuking our tumours
as though we were not in the room with them.

Say instead 'We are afraid,'
and 'We do not understand.'

Think of it as a window
misted with sighs,
not an arm wrestle with God
who sees your thoughts from afar.

Pray in tongues by all means,
but also remember our kids.
Pray that we sleep.

Pray for the obvious.
Pray we live to see Christmas.

Don't you dare
say 'It's not fair.'
Spare me your weeping.
Try saying 'Shit happens.'

The Room With No Windows

was all doors.
Outside, the ring road,
a playground.

Beyond, a field,
one calf
suckling its mother,

Atlantic rain
shrouding everything,
even the radio

in the corner,
Grade 1 piano
to an old man's singing.

Lost

Lost my hair
Lost my appetite
Lost my energy
Lost my nails

Lost my nerve
Lost my eyebrows
Lost my patience
Lost my pubes

Lost my cool
Lost my taste
Lost my lashes
Lost my faith

Lost my blood
Lost my colour
Lost my temper
Lost my hair

Men Who Sit in Waiting Rooms

alone or with their wives
tutting at old copies of *OK!*

who ignore the wig catalogues
and study the ceiling tiles

their shoes the microscopic dust
on their fingernails

who fidget with zip-pulls
on outdoor jackets

who are called
through doors down corridors

who stride without looking backwards
past the pot plants

handed a gown
told to wait

who curse that list
by the telly

those jobs
the weeds or the guttering

one perhaps for a pro
if they could lay their hands

on the number
if they could remember that name

When You Woke Up This Morning

You probably did not think
you would end up here, at this poem,
unless you have read it before,
returning to be entertained again
at the way I describe it as a raft
the two of us set sail on

without map or knowledge of the stars,
the way it suddenly becomes
an empty bedroom with a note
on the pillow saying 'Have gone out
for a walk. Back after lunch.
Have left phone behind so no point calling.'

Wart

You're not much fun,
are you, wart?
You sit there
on my finger-hinge, proudly.

Announcements
aren't your style.
Rather, you insinuate,
fattening stealthily.

Little Uluru, time-bomb,
capsule from another planet:
you glare up at me,
a word made flesh.

Words

Large cell

high grade

growth

Persistent

active

disease

Confirmed

bulky

mass

Percentage

treatable

tough

Homeshopping

Today I am homeshopping,
getting one-click fixes
from albums and fleece-lined robes.

I shall float in linen trousers,
shirts with no collars,
suede loafers.

You can keep your *Eat to Beat Cancer,*
Your *Recipes for a Longer Remission.*
I deserve

a digital radio,
a subscription to *Woman and Home* –
but I'll need the *Chemotherapy for Dummies.*

What Not to Say

Enough of your *lovely shaped head,*
your *meaning to ring.*

Tell me as it is:
I look like a waxwork.

Spare me your *positive mindset,*
your *fight it, you know you're a fighter.*

I couldn't care which website you visited
explaining it really clearly.

And you could try not calling me brave.
Invite me to dinner.
                              Offer me water.

I am Fighting

I am fighting
we are talking
in a room
across a table

You are waiting
I am fighting
down a corridor
in an armchair

You are reading
in a ward
across the bed
where I am fighting

I am sleeping
imagining dreaming
flying running
I am fighting

I am waking
stretching yawning
on the sofa
you are crying

We are walking
through a doorway
I am sitting
now I'm lying

I am sleeping
you are sitting
we are waiting
I am fighting

Heads

Toss me a black woollen polo-neck
and I become a poor man's Blofeld
developing a world-threatening virus.

Hand me those retro headphones
and I'm thoughtful Brian Eno
finishing off a new mix.

I'm Kojak without his lollipop,
a paunchy Duncan Goodhew and haggard
Syd Barrett on his bike. Bike. Give me my bike.

The Year of Drinking Water

At first I didn't mind.
All those gallons had a point;
even if I peed all night
I felt I was doing my bit.

I gulp towards my future,
drunk with hope. I raise it to the light
and see myself staring back
bent double, inside out.

I am Becoming My Grandmother

The way I dine on bread,
could live on nothing else.

The way I call *à table*
and tut to no one, shrugging,
when they don't appear
for minutes.

The way I pull at this bread,
sip coffee, and live
on nothing else.

How I stay in one room,
quite happy.
How I nod during grace
and mean it.

How I stoop.

Man in a Fleece

I disappear into grey folds,
its soft creases of flesh
which match my own.

I turn up the collar
and shuffle to the shops
for milk, the paper I will not read.

Next to you in the queue
I could be anyone,
someone fit, a jogger.

I stroke my second skin.
It catches the light in beads
which ripple up then down my arms.

Blood

in memory of Jörn Cann

The nurse announces the canula.
One *Sharp scratch* and you're there,

vial after ochre vial,
unstoppable.

Cousin to tawny port
your sheen's a glossy russet.

You do not gush, you seep,
but would soak

the world
if you could.

You're not much to look at:
but, spun, you separate –

lymph, plasma
and marrow, the very core

of us, telling everything.
Famously salty

to the taste, you seem stable as mercury.
If only.

The Young

They're beautiful, aren't they, the young?
They are loyal and walk with their heads up.

They shout their gossip in the street
and think we can't hear or are interested.

They eat and drink on the move
discarding the wrappers in the breeze.

They arrange to meet at the weekend
in at least three different formats.

They are great at sex, slamming doors,
and impulsively boarding trains.

May they discover Keats, busk in Paris.
May they look at photos exclaiming 'My God!'

I wish them a future without corridors.
I wish them cake.

Chemotherapy

after Annie Leibovitz

The world is a hillock of pillows,
a New York skyline of cards.

★

You sip at something hot
reminding yourself of its taste
by reading, re-reading the label.

★

You gorge on banana sandwiches
with sugar, cream cheese and smarties.

★

There is a play about you
on the radio.   It is everything you can do
not to pick up the phone.

★

On bad days you long to be dead.
On good days you think you are.

★

Eventually you give in to it.
You think *Yes, I could do that*
and add it to your wish list.

More Chelsea Than Sunderland

for Humphrey Potts

Your doctor's line predicting
    your survival
        tickled me

watching Terry lift the trophy
    before the World Cup
        debacle

inevitable as May following April
    thinking *I should be happy*
        imagining

that champagne moment

Spooning Couple

after Ron Mueck

The night
     of the news

        we lay
    not touching

or talking
     your arms

       folded
   across you

mine
   bent in

       wordless
    prayer   imagining

being dead
    without you

       the bed
   now twice

as big
    stranded

      in all
   that space

The End of the Affair

When you finally left me
I didn't know what to do.
As in all the best clichés
you had become my identity.

We said goodbye
 – let's hope it's not *au revoir* –
as we said hello
in a room with a desk and tissues.

I thought I wouldn't miss you
but I do.
Not you personally, but the attention
was nice.

My days grow fat without you.
There are rumours of gales
No, I don't think we can be friends.
I would rather you didn't write.

Jesus Heals Ten Lepers

for Michael Symmons Roberts

We miss just about everything.
An AIDS ward doesn't come close;

or even an oncology unit
with its scarf-headed goitred women

and men with purple necks.
Think of a family tree:

there's a blank where your name resided;
the no-go area of town: that's home.

You despise those you live with,
the stumpy whitening flesh,

the stink of rot they can't feel.
Don't even think of 'community'.

This was evidence of sin –
yours or the mother who disowned you

who in any case was known as a whore.
Even the healing command

– *show yourselves to the priest* –
is cruel, a joke, surely, pre-Python.

You can imagine how the returner felt.
He must have gripped

Jesus' ankles till they bled.
You would think he couldn't wait to leave.

Poem Beginning With a Line by Milosz

A day so happy.
I made coffee and wrote for two hours.
There were no emails to answer,
the children had cycled to town.
Two books arrived through the letterbox;
the pleasure pulsed thorough my veins.
I ate a sandwich then slept.

I dreamed of grass,
that X had finally forgiven me.

Waking, I watched apples drop
in the breeze. Wasps
gathered round the cracks
in their skins, swollen now like lips.

Prayer

Let the healing start.
May it begin in the blood
and flood every cell with light.
May it infect the heart.

(Let the healing start.)
May it come as one comforts
a newborn at midnight
the wild shocking eye closing.

(*Let it come.*) Let it start
now as we sit here waiting
and talking through days
of colour and rain.

May it infect the heart
and save it. May it lead us
into light. (We are open.)
Let the healing start.

Two

All Lives, All Dances, All is Loud

All Lives, All Dances, All is Loud

in memory of and after Lucy Mason

You take a forager's song and still it,
the tourists of a certain age and teenagers

with worksheets barely pausing
to look up this Tuesday in October,

two months into your cancer
and one day out of mine,

the sunlight in the stairwell
making everything and nothing precious.

Is what remains our story?
We learn a skill and perform it daily,

out of sight. Only afterwards
can we say *She gazed through water*

and through it saw the riverbed, the sky,
and in this way make our lives official,

as family anecdote or gesture –
he couldn't change a plug for toffee,

she never got her cakes to rise –
hardens into truth we nod at

like acquaintances from the self-same past
or children we grew up with,

unsure of what to say or whether
to offer a handshake,

keen to make an impression,
aware that it will not last –

which our own children
will choose to remember and describe

as What It Was Like and How We Lived Then:
those cheap liqueurs last thing at night,

hot cross buns on Easter Sunday only,
that holiday outside a French cathedral town

where you almost learned the name
of the local way with lamb

and the secret of cooking it slowly
when you returned home.

The past affords us these luxuries
of looking back and inventing

new-minted previous selves,
as though that shy boy

beside the *Tour Eiffel*
(you took a long detour back)

and that gap-toothed girl
in a skirt which started out

as homework then grew
into a summer-long passion

to leave the dusty suburbs,
had some part in changing

who you are or power over
who you decide they were,

arbitrary as fashion
and briefer than those foreign tans.

Step back from them
grinning on the mantelpiece

and look outside to the beyond
that is a solitary person walking

to a hurriedly-made appointment
or news which, good or bad,

cannot be received in silence;
look at them: a living

repository of hopes and nightmares
we may never encounter

or see again, their story far
from ours as that cathedral spire.

You do not need me to tell you
one beholding other is all we require

for communion to take place,
a person, we may say, of peace,

who after perhaps a lifetime's
study or sudden pang

in their gut comprehends completely
who we are and what we say

through these few innocent marks
which no one made us make.

That we live for
such connection is not a choice:

the ideas we name 'ideas'
are born in wordless rhythms;

it is more like they have us,
possessing solid properties —

the car as entrapment
metaphor; cells 'defenceless

as milk' — we could not
have dreamed or willed

until that moment of decision,
the being lost we long for.

We call it a performance
but know that it is thousands.

To move your rags to riches
takes love of your material

and unconscious design;
at some point the whole

takes over, stitched in time
and joyously outside it,

with no point but in itself
until its done, alchemy

you did not know you knew,
a feast from scraps.

And while you worked,
those 'defenceless' cells

were also busy multiplying,
tissue which forgot to die

seizing its driven moment
to set another story going,

the one which competes with this,
your real and hidden work

made public,
score of a rootless jig.

Everything points to now,
painstaking warp and weft,

your race against time,
not so much a record of events

as the main event itself
needing nothing (but grateful

to this sunlight
the day takes back as dusk),

not even success, noted
in your padlocked diary

and in letters to far-off friends
as the air of being known

by those who can discern
that your hunger arises

not from self but in wanting
to see completion

hover for a moment
before settling like dust.

So you step into your exhaustion
which is also a release,

a planet of unplanned
thought laid bare,

should we choose to look.
It will have to be enough.

The gates of the academy,
protected by powerful women

you so wanted to impress,
may or may not swing open:

each night, after work, did
you put this from your mind,

the hope that archivists
would one day beat a path

to the snug south west
and pronounce that it was in this museum

'The Bravadistes' took their coffee,
their arguments about style

now like a sepia photograph
the tourists buy postcards of?

(They needed each other
more than history,

grieving over poets they loved
but could not sustain friendships with,

the playwrights and painters
who heard their call to arms

but were never persuaded by;
is art a mere backdrop to this,

a prettifying *jeu d'esprit*
which enters the city's gossip

as one writer stabbing another
in a journal no one reads?)

Your struggle is still with air,
but of the kind that's rented

and not so faithful.
The lungfuls we take for granted,

the breath each day exhales,
swim invisibly around us,

plainer than life and less noticed
than anything we might say:

this statement beyond words
which may one day hang

in wards where we sit hairless,
a colour and life-filled space

we find ourselves reflecting in
yet is not mirror.

I imagine your routine,
but, like speaking about sex,

dare not frame it with
the distracting noise of guesswork.

I know this: you turned up
and it happened.

What you hummed each day
while working, or said across the table

at lunch (or if there *was* a lunch)
I have no idea,

an approximated myth
that is, finally, an insult,

like those well-read friends
only fascinated by poets

they can put a name to
('He *really* slept with *her*?')

which even then is inaccurate,
their work a rumour distant

as New York with its famed 'people
of the air'. I also know this:

a guard checked his watch
on being asked the time

and somewhere in the basement
a bell rang for us to leave.

I meant to go back, but didn't.
I shall not see it again.

Now you are public property
that's similarly silent:

we track the progress
of your cells' rebellion

as though that's your only story.
If and when I pray

it's not for your fame
but that your loved ones knew

you lived the other life –
daydreaming hard while cooking

or pulling out of scrapbooks
from before their time

small threads whose purpose
you could not have predicted:

the gateway signs of tramps
in notched fence-posts,

now a shimmering dream
you say 'made itself'

outliving them and us,
like those distant cathedral bells

tolling three seconds
behind the time we live by

and insisting: 'That small handful
of life, how did you use it?'

Three

Riddance

The Clothes I Bought During Cancer

were soft and wrinkle-free
shrouding my yellowing skin
and expanding waistline
in billowy folds
rendering them invisible as after giving birth.

Though I would struggle for breath on their stairs
I shuffled along shop-front shadows,
ogling drawstring trousers
and collarless cheesecloth shirts
with stripes I hoped were slimming.

Doubletake after doubletake
I'd catch myself staring back
as if waiting for the flash at a wedding,
my grin so compliant it hurt,
my hair short for fashion not necessity.

Diagnosis

And while you cried, well,
I went completely numb,

a foretaste of what to expect
wired up to the needle,

my arm cold
to the marrow,

which is where the problem was,
as though I had disappeared.

Playing Dead

I lie on the flagstone table
as they count off my numbers in code.

My insides are melting like chocolate.
A red beam falls into my eye.

'What a Feeling' plays on the radio.
They ask if I have plans for the weekend.

In the corner sits a teddy.
He stays with me during the buzzing.

If I even itch my nose
we will have to *start from scratch*.

The last time I lay this still
I was playing at being dead.

They're right, you really don't feel a thing.
I breathe in *and hold*, like a good boy.

The Other Life

in memory of Emily Riall

I want to wake up in a house
where the ghosts have recently departed,

persuaded to leave by prayer
infused with wordless singing,

its roomy silences punctuated
by waves and far-off bells.

I want to visit a village,
its market infecting the alleyways

with tables groaning with cheeses,
gossip and outdoor coffee,

where they call me my childhood nickname;
may I know and taste the air there,

a whiff of salt and apples,
a backnote of conker and dog;

and may it be endlessly Saturday,
the bonfires yet to start drifting towards the blue.

November

Today is a day of softly-spoken men
in flower shops, the backwoods tang

of newsagents nobody visits,
of seafront chip shops shutting up early,

a day of small change, dated gossip,
and glances across cafés

once brilliantly lit ballrooms,
now anxious of staying open

just one more season, the tourists gone,
the upmarket couples back at work.

It is a day to test even the dog walkers
as they lean into the wind,

the river too choppy for swans
and warnings far up the estuary,

of deciding to remain indoors,
the world shrunk to a teaset

and rain needling the windows
before it has a chance to grow light.

Doctor Evil Has Plans For World Domination

but the smell of pastries throws him
halfway down Corridor F,
his bowels suddenly like jelly.

He tried blasting the factory from space –
instead it is his turn to be zapped.
His bones will be luminous for days.

Naked as a baby on the table
he admires the machine's disregard
for his feelings.

That woman in the blue mask and gloves:
if only he could unlock her smile
the world would be his, his, all his.

No

the only agelessness is yes

-Brendan Kennelly

I refuse you as one does
the offer of eating mud.

Life and love and yes
share your count in syllables

but oppose your thud
in the throat presaging death.

You repulse me, choice-
killer, slayer of movement,

sucker of breath from voice
and all things not imprisoned,

alive in their moment
of growth and towards.

I hate your rejection
of maybe, your strangling

of perhaps. When you arrive
pulse leaves, banning all decision

for joy. You do not live
in these bones, your hands were never mine.

The Hand

after Michael Donaghy

We hold on to what we can.
The evening fades, grows weak and
dies, as I will one day, surely, a man
like any other but that you held my hand,

held dear what fell into your hand,
this briefly gripping flesh which can
pretend it holds the future, as a man
knows his mirror-self's fake and

always will be. If I could I would hand
you the future; would claim I can
live into it. Instead I'm –just– man
enough to know that I know nothing and

cannot change. And yet. And
yet: we hold on to what we can;
a fast-disappearing man
locks fingers: in giving he loses his hand.

They Said About the Tiredness

and the nausea and the hairloss
and the diarrhoea/constipation
and the sore gums and the tingling
in the ends of the fingers/toes
and the shivers and the Big Bone Pain
and the metallic taste in the mouth
and/or the loss of taste altogether
the loss of desire for alcohol
the possible depression and the headaches
and the cracking of the fingernails
and the intolerance to certain smells
and the steroids giving one moodswings
and the need to drink three litres of water
and the need for the family to talk
and the need to stay out of the sun
and the afterburn of persistent fatigue
which is normal
even the sheer relief
but they never said about getting better

Probably Nothing

It's probably nothing
    most likely benign.
It isn't, it's cancer.
    There isn't much time.

But you're brave,
    you'll beat it, they said.
You don't know anything.
    I wish I were dead.

It sounds just like pregnancy.
    (It suits you, you know.)
You've no idea.
    I think you should go.

You won,
    you beat it, they say.
No I didn't.
    But it did go away.

Summer

When the music stops
I shall still be sitting here

in the shade of the apple tree
amazed by the play

of light on the raspberries
grateful to the poppy-nodding breeze.

In the time it takes two ants
to climb the face of my knee cap

I shall offer a gulp of praise –
the gardens stunted by heat

and the afternoon now silent
but for the slurring of bees

and one speculative blackbird
calculating the maze

of hedges and catcalls
unsure how to navigate home.

To the Programmers of Daytime Television

What exactly were you thinking
when you filled our waiting rooms
with *ER* and *Holby City* reruns?

Did you really think
our cancers would panic and vanish
at the sight of *Diagnosis Murder*,

that somehow we'd feel better
after *Through the Keyhole, How to Live Longer, Flog It!?*
What we need is beyond mindless:

Dangermouse, Whacky Races, The Hair Bear Bunch.

A Few Odds and Sods

was all he said I'd need:
'It's only overnight.'

I hated the midnight obs,
the moaning and tossing of men

who didn't know where they were,
offering to buy everyone drinks.

Just dozing off at six
a trolley appeared with tea.

I told them my birth-date
and got seen last.

The scan on my balls was fun:
'Just like a pair of lychees.'

They booked in a day for more tests.
Then came the visitors and the grapes.

Jem Southam's Photographs

Your stills on
'Hospital Road'

        – home of trolleys
and draughts –

        live on in jokes
porters make,

        gaze squarely
at what's loved

        and missed daily:
the things

        in front of us
at supper,

        a baby
eyeballing

        a tomcat
for one second,

        a glance up,
nothing more,

        looking, like you,
looking still.

For Afterwards

I want it kept simple.
I want to leave one part
of the congregation
thinking they witnessed
a jazz improvisation,

another they attended
a poetry reading
and another that a sermon
wasn't preached at all—
the kind I long to hear still,

including a story
about a boy and a boat,
a mention of the Prodigal Son,
and a metaphor
concerning train drivers.

I'll have no wisdom
from the other side.
I direct you instead
to the cracker-jokes
buried in my best suit,

the postcard I keep
for emergencies, blank
but for the words:
'That green notebook
was a good time of life.'

Day Case

After the aeon
    in the waiting room
each of us differently afraid
    some pacing to become invisible

the years
    of bacon sandwiches
those post-roast trifle Sundays
    blurring but etched in our frowns

we turn
    at out-of-date pages
depicting if-only holidays
    and impossibly perfect interiors

like housewives
    enduring a morning
at the hairdressers
    patient in a row on our drips

Offline

Today I am deleting emails.
Goodbye Dead Cheap Viagra,
Performance Development Review,
Research Assessment Exercise.

Even How Are You? gets short shrift:
It's big,
I exist,
not like I had a choice.

What really hurts:
they assume I've lost my appetite for gossip.
She called him what *at that meeting?*
Go on, tell me again. Tell me till I'm sick.

On Re-reading 'The Man With Night Sweats'

Today is Valentine's.
Later they will tell me
what I know in my bones.
It will not be pretty.

Shivering and soaked through
I'm put in mind of you

pacing the floor at dawn,
listening for avalanche
in sinew and in skin
which do not seem to change;

and yet you know full well
how skin feels when it melts,

the sabotage of cells
destroying their good host
while dining out in hell.
Our plagues are cousins, ghost:

the curse within our blood
can never be proved good.

Your rhymes dare me to dream –
not of eternal life,
that things aren't what they seem –
of living in the light

long enough to be brave.
May it never arrive.

Lists

This is where I shop.
And this is how much it costs.

I do the washing on Mondays.
This is where I hang it.

The food I keep in here.
It is all clearly labelled.

The number for the bank is here.
(They know me by my first name.)

I set off early with the boys.
Give yourself plenty of time.

What you do with the day is yours.
I find the radio a great help.

And this is how I die.
This is how you help me.

On Dying

It really didn't hurt.
Like what they say about drowning
only kinder, less panicky.

What's weird is that you go on being there
in the room with them,
right under their noses.

None of the noise
brings you back, though.
It can get quite annoying.

When all the fuss has died down
everything just carries on.
You still turn up for work, the shopping.

You might spot me by the bread
or in the library
trying to look anonymous.

I wouldn't advise pointing
or asking if you know me from somewhere.
It's a bit late for that now, don't you think.

My Toenail in Madrid

after Julia Darling

flattened out
   like a knife
pretended to be hard-edged
   again
treated itself to socks

     decided
it could be a diving board

bled a little
   was nervous

   stood
in a bar munching olives
managed
   not to get pissed

     believed it had the answer

stepped into a puddle
   felt sick
longed for a banana

   slept badly
but didn't snap off

   swallowed
Paracetamol
     for luck

shouted
    sod it, let's take a taxi
          left

too big a tip
    didn't tip nearly
    enough

watched schoolkids
    listening to Miro

was lazy

    quoted from the guidebook
in the street
      shrugged and
          laughed
in the Rastro
translated everything
    literally
    walked much further than
expected

slunk back at all hours

    was
    almost
      flattened by a nun

loved *Guernica*
and the Goyas

even *The Triumph of Death*

Visitation

Imagine walking
for a year
down a tunnel

the exit
a tale
you hear rumours of

the survivors
few
but ecstatic

their story
not yours
in the papers

Now imagine
the darkness
thickening

a cataract
on your eyes
like lichen

then suddenly
finding yourself
blinded

the faultline
in a cloud
breaking open

the feet
of its column
standing

where you stand
within its hologram
of light

Riddance

What kept us going or sane
could be Col's Jamie Oliver Bolognese
(for afters a tub of Cherry Garcia)
we'll always associate with cancer.

Or, what we say we want to forget's
in the end what made it bearable –
those vigils in the kitchen over coffee
when really there wasn't much to discuss

a test that in normal life isn't one
what happens when you're not looking
or looking the other way
nice though that is sometimes, beautiful even.

The Land of What Next

Everyone needed to touch me,
that's what I noticed.
I couldn't blame them.
After all, they'd cheered as I swam
through concrete to get there.

They looked so disappointed
when I told them
there was nothing to see,
one hairless oblong on my tummy,
another of sunburn on my back.

I was invited to big houses
where I provided entertainment
by standing on my head
in glass cages
drinking champagne through my nose.

Eventually the parties dried up.
I noticed if I walked anywhere
it still took forever. Aren't you angry,
they said. No, I said.
Why on earth would I feel that?

Borderline

for and after Lawrence Sail

the sump-life of the place

-*Seamus Heaney*

These are the flatlands
stitched between flood-plain and ditch,

everything provisional,
ooze and sluice.

The estuary looks walkable,
spines of red clay

rising from slate water
with flanks of weeping slip

which shimmer mother-of-pearl,
silver, molten.

A powerboat that was toy
bounces through its roar,

its wake slapping
the cledge, scattering wagtails.

The stranded barge
of The Turf breathes easy,

its spur both tongue
and poop-deck.

Beyond, a train
becomes its horn;

skeletal willows inch greener;
and an oarsman

pushes himself backwards
into the future.

The Quiet Room

for Louise Page

Where Jörn told us what a hickman line was,
what the next steps were, their chances,
and 'If you're handed a shit pack of cards
that's what you have to play with';
where nine days later there was a knock,
then a suit, then a whisper,
a letter brandished in silence,
my results now wrong in the right way,
how it might have happened, what that meant;
where now I come out of choice,
every week if I could, and for free,
going beyond myself in questions
all in confidence, one drug
I don't want to be weaned off;
where, from nowhere, I find myself praising
those smokers at the gates,
their banished impromptu coteries
of cleaner, auxiliary and line manager
offering a light in all weathers, especially
the one-legged gent on crutches
sticking two fingers to the traffic.

Acceptance

for Mark H

Like when we lay awake
discussing where I'd buried
the paperwork for the ISAs
and which music I wanted played,

this, I'm told, is a phase,
that it's normal,
important to wonder
What if and *Was it really me?*,

take time choosing what next from now,
though that's never been my strong suit,
from sweets to record shops to Christmas,
though how I'd put it is

really a friend of a friend's
definition of happiness: you take
away what a man has, give it back,
then watch his face for news.

Cured

for Marilyn Pocock

Today I am bright-boned
fizzing through puddles on my bike,
helmeted, luminous-fingered, tanned,
in love with life,

the play of shadow and light,
warm, making plans
and looking back at myself as one might
an intruder who took the money and ran.

Four

Three Lifetimes

I have been standing on estuary sands.
The sky comes to gossip and stretch.

A bus of white heads and coats.
A blue tractor, taller than me.

The charcoal outline of a farm
with two brushstrokes of washing.

There are four buds on this hawthorn.
The wind is not an old woman shrieking.

My day churns on,
light fading under the bridges
and beneath the disused railway
where lately I have stood watching
trains slice the park with their clatter,
the swings trembling like tuning forks
in the pink dusk now strewn
with litter and prams.

One of the weirder nights.
At four the boy came in
and snuggled down between us –
gangly meteorite, with elbows.

Then, voices from the street
or in here, I couldn't tell,
warning all sorts,
brake failure, flooding, a plague of lemons.

At dawn, with government defeat and coffee
a spider snared an insignificant looking fly.
Beyond, out of focus, our kale plants,
shot, suddenly, and stooping.

Some things are too close to mention –
X's weight loss, the sudden death of Y.

And yet, today was special:
serviceable hot choc at the station

and there, a display of children's art.
A poet had taken them to the coast.

The beaks of the birds they saw blazed orange,
a collage of their chopped up tickets.

The garage for instance,
where my walking boots
are already growing mould
in the space under the guinea-pig hutch.

I pull open a drawer – it's full
of rotted bulbs. A woodlouse
scuttles away, put out
at the interruption.

And these rusting shears
should be somewhere dry,
not this junkshop of the damned
with only a lightbulb for company.

The kitchen table today –
a pile of bills, old papers
and letters about school trips.
From the left the poem nudges me

and I am out on the ring road
with the lorry-spray, cursing my saddle
and praying my brakes will hold.
The physio said I had good muscle tone.

Small consolation when I forget
to buy bread or call the electrician.
I remember you, he will say.
We did your plugs and you was happy.

The real reason for working –
being able to buy books
and a pint of Otter for Jonathan
without worrying

The same goes for bass leads
a vocal mike
and that PJ Harvey
Mart convinced me he needed

Now I just need time
to read it all, take it all in
These lines from a *Collected*
I've ignored since July:

The corms come by mail, are planted,
then do their thing: to live! To live!

We found the waterfall
at the end of the track
on the right angle bend
three bridges before the village.

We found clichés there:
hidden depths, a tyre on a rope.
Also, fragments of bottle,
blackened stones.

What they said was true:
the house was haunted
by the ghosts of servants'
children conceived in attics
during storms.

They would appear each Whitsun,
stooping to pour the laird
an imaginary whisky
before he retired to his chilly quarters
muttering about money.

'Give us our freedom,' they said,
'and we shall leave this place in peace'.
But he would have none of it,
sending them packing with his horsewhip,
his eyes veined like Stilton.

Before work —three lifetimes:
sous chef, taxi, binman
(not to mention the others),

plus distant friend to this postcard
from Bruges where the chips are hot
and the wood carvings quite out of this world

Another disastrous meal.
I mishear 'phone' for 'coat',
am not granted a retelling.

A hearty winter soup,
onions sweated properly with cumin.

They pronounce it delicious
thanking me without looking back.

The pile of magazines
in the bathroom
reveals when I kick it by accident
a poet I have not spoken to in years.

I love his work –
I wrote to tell him.
Somewhere, life intervened
and our conversation stalled.

In the paper is a free CD,
another is a clothing catalogue.
I'm ashamed
even to have them.

But not nearly as much as this,
bought at a station,
with its Bargain Bikinis
and Colour Clash Accessories supplement.

The house ticks.
What I thought
was an upstairs radiator
was actually my own plumbing
gurgling in the darkness.
I am not a clever man
nor a good one.

Two pencil-lines of light
either side of the blind
give definition to the room
allowing me time to notice your tights
draped on the laundry basket,
one leg tucked safely inside,
the other still struggling to join it.

The week lies ahead like a tunnel:
Monday: science tutoring,
Tuesday: rugby practice,
Thursday: the dentist's.

In the silent kitchen
my hand pauses
on the radio dial,
the kettle switch clicks.

If I make tea
it will be one kind of week;
if I put on a news programme,
the other.

Raw March winds
send bluetits scattering
into the bare branches
of the apple tree.

If they survive this
they can live through anything,
even my ineptitude,
the bird feeder swaying half empty.

It is two years since you died,
friend I miss more than I dare imagine.

I don't know what they have to show
for themselves – I'm guessing

that you might from above,
or wherever it is you are hiding.

I am fine, since you ask. I'm fine.
I live with pain, which I couldn't before,

only some of which is sourced in your absence,
some of which my anger at the same.

What is inside these bodies
we have been given?

My grandmother cut down at 90,
my mother shrinks each day.

Sister knee, have you come for me too?
Cousin leukaemia, you look oddly familiar.

Or good old grandfather heart attack,
reliable as eye colour, harder than bone.

Last night there were storms:
several times I woke up to see
if our fence had made it.

I needn't have worried:
here are Roy's Heath Robinson supports
and the garden he'll sing opera
to later, sharper than a razor.

I'm stuck in traffic when I see them
through the sleeting rain, in a gaggle.
He's grinning like an idiot,
she's laughing with her head back.

I'm just admiring her cheek-bones –
so delicate, pale and high –
when I realise it's her.
And then that they're holding hands.

I move off as they pass the car
but not before our eyes meet,
the girl I make breakfast for
after asking how she slept.

These poems have been arriving each day.
They're not what I expected to write.

Anything is allowed: sunlight on a fruit-bowl,
the washing line's pearls after rain.

You want to say *thank you* or *thank you, God*
at such times, grateful though you were before.

The bats wheel at head height
as jazz blares from the barn.

Shivering on the gravel
we knock back another Merlot,

link arms and declaim
our faith in the daydream.

For a second the stars are reachable,
living in stopped time.

Five

Reasons for Life

It's Changed

on the ward where they filled me
with life-saving chemicals
which made my hair fall out.

Denise is wearing make-up.
There is brown toast in the café.

We discuss the important things,
like the weather,
but never what happens here,
the binging of the drips.

Jörn would have hated it.
He'd say it was too fucking quiet
and why weren't we dead yet,
didn't we have homes to go to?

The doctors seem younger.
One of them leans on a wall
reading someone's chart
in what looks like a nightie.

We Introverts

Are expert at faking it,
the life and soul one minute,
stepping out in the next
for a cigarette
and catching the ocean in an oak,
grateful to be brought back to size.

We protect the silence at our core
with perfectly improvised chatter
and long to be home.
We find one person to share this with,
secretly hoping our children
are not similarly infected.

Teacups

for Harriet Mitchell-Riall

How you fit with me
is our shared history,
as, on winter afternoons
with Marmite and toast,
we tell our secrets

looking out to sea
cradling cups that contain
silence, and, cupping them,
saucers, flat in the palm,
open to the weather.

Seller Feedback

The Selected Poems of Robert Bringhurst

How is this acceptable?
How is it? This savaged man
of a book, with its cracked spine,
its deep fissures running in opposing lines,
through the author's name? How?
Is it a joke? It is concave in my palm.
It is a cradle, a shell,
a fragment of shrapnel –
it seems a juggernaut has run over it
or a strong-man tried to tear it apart.
How is it 'acceptable'?
It creaks as I turn its pages,
they are a valley frowning up at me,
dented, scarred as if greeted
by a blade of great velocity.
Is this an 'acceptable' 'condition'?
It trembles in my hand; it wobbles;
it breathes its last.
Perhaps it is a prank
or form of conceptual art.
Think of it: someone saw fit
first to attack, then package it
for meagre profit, its outline horned,
even through the jiffy bag, this
fallen angel, broken bird,
amputated wing, falling
onto my doormat,
torn and moaning beast
speaking in the voices of others
come back from the earth.

The Honest Truth

I love it when people ask about my health.
Not 'How are you?' or 'How are you *really*?'
but 'Tell me how you're keeping. You look terrific,
by the way.' Sometimes they touch my arm.
I want to kiss them on the forehead,
wash their feet with my tears, massage
their pores with pure nard, a towel strapped
to my waist. I want to promise them stars,
unbroken skies, blossom mirrored in a lake.

I do not think they want to know
about the wave of ice making its way
up my arm, be reminded of bone pain,
the hours I sometimes lose gazing into space
wondering if I will ever recover or reach a stage
when this will leave or make sense.
I think they want to know I am happy,
that I wake and face each day with gratitude,
or at least am returning to who I was before.

There is a pause as I look into their eyes,
these kind people who cooked meals,
gave lifts, sat in silence as they watched me
make coffee in return for their flowers.
I thank them and say I am fine. Relieved,
pleased to have been of help, they leave.
I cannot tell them what they do not want to hear.
The honest truth is I did not disappear, but think
I did, sometimes, and want to, even though I look terrific.

Poem Beginning With a Line by Jaan Kaplinski

This morning was cold, but it warmed about mid-day.
I left everyone eating a late breakfast,
returned to an empty house,
pretty much tidy, a miracle.
I swept for a while, hung washing
then realised it was past lunch.
I sat outside with a sandwich, the paper spread
on the table in the style of my grandfather,
cricket on the radio in the style of my father.
In the manner of my mother I hung more washing.
England were safe. I could have sat there forever,
sun on my neck, sheets flapping,
no one to answer to.
Coming back from the bakery I saw Andy looking tanned.
We leaned on our wall for a while swapping stories
about our summers. An old woman came past
and asked for the number of my builder.
Bending to write it in her notebook
I couldn't help noticing her handbag
contained the most appalling odour of tomcat.

On Speaking to One Another from Different Rooms

Distorted and lingering, 'Ant!, Dad!, Tats!'
grow interchangeable, explosive,
each sounding furious,
A search for keys in one room
nourishes fear of lateness in another.
From a kettle filled and boiling
to the weather, daily noise is damned
for drowning the needs of *now!*
My reply is weapon and filibuster,
deliberate *sotto voce,* below war level,
another trait of my father
I will never perfect:
I'm here, Can't hear you, What is it?,
screaming inside 'Who died?'
Because everything is not where we left it
history will revisit us tomorrow
at approximately the same time.
The door is almost closed
and we have not said our goodbyes yet.

Golf at Hawick

for Jock Encombe and Mark Pougatch

Or as we have learned to call it,
The Vertish: Vale of Unending Pain,
seasickness crossed with vertigo
at three-footers blown back uphill
by avenging winds from Oslo;

where you can play a back-door loop
for a fiver, watch blizzards
maze across heathland below you,
materialize and vanish between shots,
crystals melting on the hailstone of your ball;

or stand on summer evenings and see
your shadow reach the High Street
teeing off at the last
into a haze of midges lit up
like seeds across a tractor-light;

and swap banter with the Voice of Rugby
or cigarette-chewing locals barking
'Tek oot ya puttah, ya numpty'
for one-in-five downhill chips
to greens like ice, which they are.

At Villars

Glaciers are mountain ice, traffic and way of life,
    the morning as aeon in the pavement café
or fashion-dissection at the boulangerie;
        where an airport *Times* lasts a week
    between spa, *chocolatier* and cashmere boutique,
        après and pre-piste bars and salons *du thé*.

Further out, in the chalet-estates, Christmas tree
    hedges separate driveway MPVs whose tyres do not see
mud. From cable cars these foursquare alpine *schlosses*
        look plonked in vertiginous competition. You emerge
    to gasp at deltas of scree, sheer from the verge,
        grateful for the restaurant with its decking and *prix fixe*.

The golf here is crazy, both toy and regular.
    Teeing off into the void, you feel you could reach Geneva.
Ditto the train, pulling on cogs in reverse, diagonal.
        And buzzards hang motionless on thermals eeking
    and echoing above shriek-provoking hairpins
        which slalom up the mountainside perfectly parallel.

To Peter Sansom From a Classroom in Exeter

It's quiet in here.
I've given them games
they are surprised by,
granted for the first time
since their schooling
permission to get it wrong,
though I tell them they can't,
my every word in notes
they will never re-read,
preferring instead these poems
they call their own because of you.
Sometimes I tell them the story,
how you said I looked cool
in my shorts in the queue
to shake your hand
behind all the offers to stay,
when all I wanted was a mag,
never dreaming of first names
with that hero now very much flesh
I see once a century
if I'm lucky. Our banter
is your wife and mine,
the kids we are famous to,
rarely poetry. On grey days
I think of you waiting
for a kettle hundreds of miles
from here, expert at the indolence
you say we need, and imagine you
bemused, the cat, say, at your ankles,
or the garden seeming darker
than before, making in noticing
the good you call use, like tea.

This happens because
one day I drove a friend
and her friend to their uni
and leaving them enjoyed
the treat of an hour in a bookshop
down a backstreet. What I found,
though finding is the tense,
was more than I bargained for,
a way of looking
and the life itself, and is me
continually, hearing myself back
but different in lines I recognised
though they were new.
I had searched for this
but had never dared let on,
not in so many words.

Helping My Son With His GCSE Poetry Homework

Built like a flanker, swearing like a football-dad
it's four Weetabix to a bowl,
Fifa scores with strangers
and show-me-the-money demands
while I search for his hoodie.

Any excuse for some joshing, he's there,
pretending the fridge is a lineout,
sending me crashing with a nudge.
But the six-year-old in him still
grabs at sweeties, Friday night treats.

His last year at primary I shuffled
to keep up with him before chemo,
his questions about death
pricking my eyes, about the time
we stopped kissing goodbye at the gates.

My First Wave

for Phil and Sam Randall

Pulsing green and aquamarine
below the surface
the breakers rear, roar
and paff you. You paddle out
and bob, expectant.
Far out they start charcoal,
invisible, then tower
cappuccino which flip you
as you turn. Resurfacing,
salt gulps into the cave of you,
under the tongue.
You might catch four in an hour.
Or none. Walking back
you grow shadow again,
lither, slinky-glistening,
feeling half your weight,
grinning longer than your board.
And a ten-year-old whizzes by
on foam the size of a house.

On 'The Exeter Poets'

after Kenneth Koch

When I wrote 'The Exeter Poets'
I felt I put everyone and everything into it

that was both tactful and possible
without giving up the neuroses

and shameful secrets
of my fellow practitioners.

While I did not receive hate mail
for my trouble

word did get around our miniscule orbit
interrogating my omissions

as much as my inclusions
—why, for example, was there no mention of Luke?

Or Alasdair, or Fiona?
(For the record, I love both Luke

and his work. And Fiona is
the best.

The truth is, Luke is not woven into my life
in the same way Andy or Lawrence are,

even though we once shared a curry
at the house of Rupert

and lived to tell the tale.
Luke is like the Sex Pistols

in that he makes you realise
that what you have been wanting to listen to

and what you have been listening to
are not the same thing at all

and that a great gulf
exists between them.

Some choose prayer as their remedy,
others the library.

You cannot know
everyone.)

Since 'The Exeter Poets' was written
many of us have been ill, or moved.

We still play in the Black Box,
graciously hosted by Tony, with James.

While I am on the subject of James
you must believe me when I say

I have no recollection which James
is which in the poem.

I love James for his diffidence,
the other for his energy.

And even now I do not know
which James I am referring to.

Against Realism

This stuff you've been giving us recently
about the fledgling flailing atop a duster
just will not do. Likewise your description
of its body: were its eyes mahogany,
I mean, actually? Also, why is its bib
a Victorian's beard? And the way you spring
it upwards, as after a slip-catch:
why must cricket keep appearing in your work?

I am anxious, too, as to your state of mind.
Questions such as Am I any good?
or How do I compare with—?
lead only to madness, jealousy and paranoia,
you must know that by now. By all means
read the beautiful poets, if you think it will help.
But you know as well as I do you often
lack sleep for days afterwards.

Go where your energy is: those who say
you found your voice too early 'perhaps'
are cretins and need spanking.
You are much funnier than you think
and much better company when you bounce!
You know you are going to die one day,
what difference will it make
if your stones don't skim perfectly?

On His Last Ever Drop of Teacher's

Today I woke up, as so often,
with nothing on my mind but you.
How many mornings have we done
that together, chatting pleasantly
swallowing Nurofen in secret?
In our early days I adored you,
could not resist you, loved how
you'd get me through parties
smiling confidently. I availed myself
of your company in many houses,
each time bouncing from bed
towards coffee with barely a shrug.
You took such care of me.
Now I am finding it hard to make
even a sandwich without you there,
as some insist on ketchup with eggs.
I try to say goodbye to you
but you lean on me promising friendship
and great energy as a lover
when all you want is my money.
Such times we have had together,
too many to count or remember.
There'll never be another like you,
you with your shouted singing,
overnight bags, your eyes like bruises.

The Ring

for Pete and Ana James

And if I said a part of me
leapt from a skyscraper
as I took your trembling finger
that would be utterly true,

each tiny syllable detonating
in my throat: *forsaking;*
till death; who had kept
a promise once, for a week,

then dined out on the story
with whoever would listen.
Your beaming smile had none of it:
Don't say a word you can't mean.

Sounding twelve and looking it
I jammed the ring onto you,
knowing nothing of honesty
except you honestly looked gorgeous.

So believe me when I say
I would stand and face you again,
promise everything a second time,
this time to savour the words.

Reasons for Life

after Mark Halliday

Because of the desks. And the luck.
And because there are too many eighteen-year-olds
running round with guns because Miss Eve said
'Not now, Darren, let's get back to the Pharaohs.'
Because: 'Not one day went by
when reading was easy.'

And because Miss Brown ignored
the sunlight, filled with dust motes,
and had you sketching shells
from her Greek holiday instead.
And in spite of Miss Janners in Geography and everyone in
                                                    Physics,
there was Mr Lee in Chemistry and Mrs Crump in Spelling.
                                                    Especially
Mrs Crump.

Because once, the classroom emptying,
the blackboard groaning with homework,
someone approached your crouching form
and said how pleased they were
you had attended their lesson
and had you considered reading Lawrence.

Because if they don't get it from you,
who will they get it from?
Because of the desks of forgetting,
the sunlight filled with dust
of wanting to be outside
and the luck of finding someone who found you interesting
enough to believe in.

Because your dad was, or mum was
and the sight of a kitchen table piled high with blue books
appeals to you in the way computers and cars
sing to those you grew up with,
who now live in suburbs you avoid
because they are full of roundabouts.

Because you burn with it,
basically,

which brings you here
to this room, just one more filled with desks and sunlight and
                                                    dust motes,
and because time means nothing to Isha, and Ashraf
is making plans to look nobody in the eye.

To My Cancer

When you left me
I did not say goodbye.

I kissed you
then carried you outside.

You did not leave.
I am still saying goodbye.